HOW TO DRAW
MACHINES

Moira Butterfield
and Anita Ganeri

Designed by Kim Blundell and Robert Walster

Illustrated by Kim Blundell, Chris Lyon, Steve Cross, Peter Bull and Graham Round

Additional designs by Steve Page

Contents

About this book

If you are interested in machines you may enjoy drawing them. This book shows you techniques for drawing all kinds of machines.

You can find out how to draw realistic pictures of machines you see around you, such as cars, trains, planes and bikes.

There are also tips on drawing cartoon machines – making them look funny and friendly, or fierce and frightening.

You can use your imagination to invent fantasy machines such as robots and spaceships. There are lots of ideas to start you off.

At the end of the book, there is a section on designing machines, using professional techniques such as "cutaways".

Drawing tips

Before you start drawing, here is some information about different drawing materials. You can find out how to use them, for instance to shade an object to make it look solid.

For sketching practice and for experimenting, you can draw on pieces of scrap paper. For more finished drawings you many want to use cartridge paper which is better quality.

Materials and shading

Paints, inks and thick felt tips give flat areas of colour. These are good for simple pictures and diagrams. Use a darker colour to do the shading.

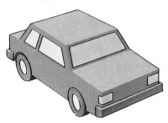

This shape is on page 4.

Copying pictures

Here is a method you can use to copy a picture. This helps you to work out how it was drawn.

Use a ruler to measure out the grid.

You could use this method to copy pictures in this book.

1 On tracing paper, draw a grid made up of equal-sized squares, like the one shown above. Make the grid large enough to cover the whole picture.

Pencils, crayons and fine felt tips give a clear outline. You can use them for hatching – a way of shading using lines.

Use straight lines to shade flat surfaces and curved lines for rounded surfaces.

Crossed lines, called cross-hatching, are used to give darker shading. This technique works well on flat surfaces.

This shape is on page 18.

This shape is on page 11.

A useful method for shading curved surfaces is to use lots of dots. This is called stippling. Use pencils, crayons or fine felt tips. The closer together the dots, the darker the shading.

This shape is on page 22.

Charcoal and chalk can be used for big pictures. You can shade by smudging the lines with your finger. You can also smudge a soft lead pencil.

This shape is on page 12.

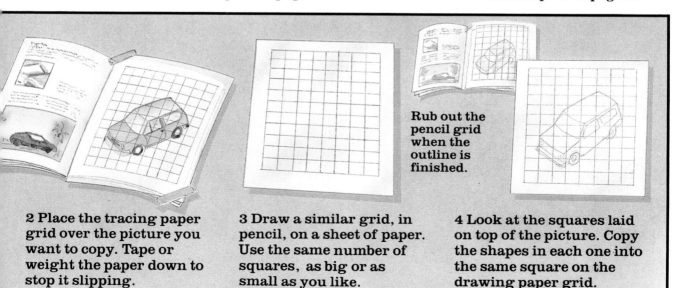

Rub out the pencil grid when the outline is finished.

2 Place the tracing paper grid over the picture you want to copy. Tape or weight the paper down to stop it slipping.

3 Draw a similar grid, in pencil, on a sheet of paper. Use the same number of squares, as big or as small as you like.

4 Look at the squares laid on top of the picture. Copy the shapes in each one into the same square on the drawing paper grid.

Cars

Cars are made up of simple shapes and are quite easy to draw. You can make them look sleek and shiny, or you can draw cartoon cars with human faces.

There are some suggestions for car pictures on the next four pages. Looking at a real car, or a photo of one, will help you to get the shapes right.

A car shape

The lines shown in pink should be parallel*.

Draw a car shape inside the boxes.

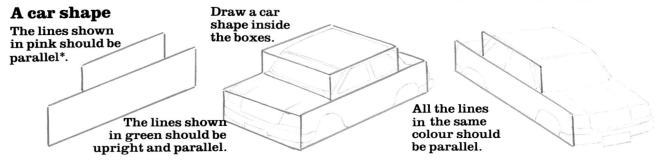

The lines shown in green should be upright and parallel.

All the lines in the same colour should be parallel.

To draw an angled view of a car, pencil in two slanting boxes like the ones above. You can rub them out later.

Add sides to the boxes to give a more solid shape. Use the boxes to help you work out the outline of your car.

If you want to vary the angle of the car, change the angle of the two boxes you begin with.

Colouring in

Once you have drawn the car shape you can colour it in and finish it off as shown here.

Draw shadowy shapes in the windows to suggest the insides of the car.

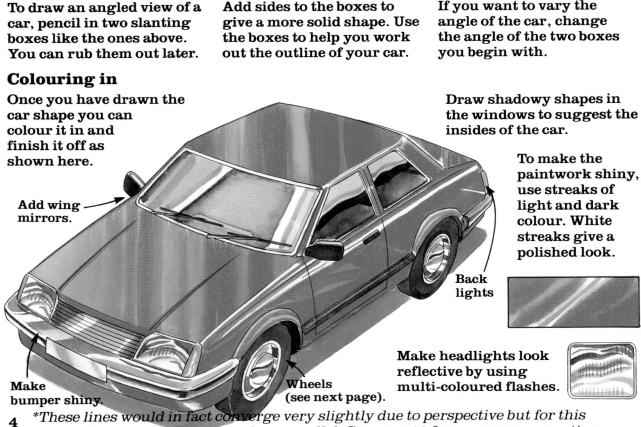

Add wing mirrors.

To make the paintwork shiny, use streaks of light and dark colour. White streaks give a polished look.

Back lights

Make bumper shiny.

Wheels (see next page).

Make headlights look reflective by using multi-coloured flashes.

4 *These lines would in fact converge very slightly due to perspective but for this simple drawing you can draw them parallel. See page 13 for more on perspective.*

Drawing a wheel

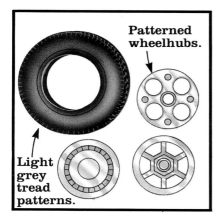

Patterned wheelhubs.

Light grey tread patterns.

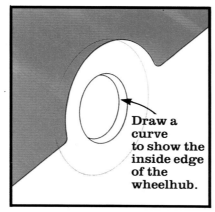

Draw a curve to show the inside edge of the wheelhub.

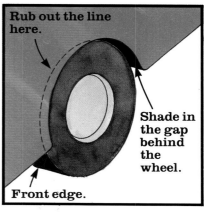

Rub out the line here.

Shade in the gap behind the wheel.

Front edge.

You can make a car tyre look rounded and full of air by using grey shading, as above. Add a light grey treadpattern and a wheelhub.

To show a wheel at an angle, draw an oval shape on the side of the car body, and draw in a smaller oval for the wheelhub.

Rub out the part of the oval that goes over the car body. Draw in the front edge of the wheel, and shade it in.

Custom cars

Some people "customize" cars as a hobby. That means they add their own special decorations to make totally original vehicles. On the right are some suggestions for you to copy or trace.

Wing mirrors

Blobmobile

Flaming speedster

Zebra Mark 1

Flower power

Sports car

Sports cars have a streamlined shape, to help them go faster. You can get this effect by starting with the shape on the right.

Wedge-shaped front

Sloping back

This car has been done in three shades of the same colour. The background and road are blurred to show speed.

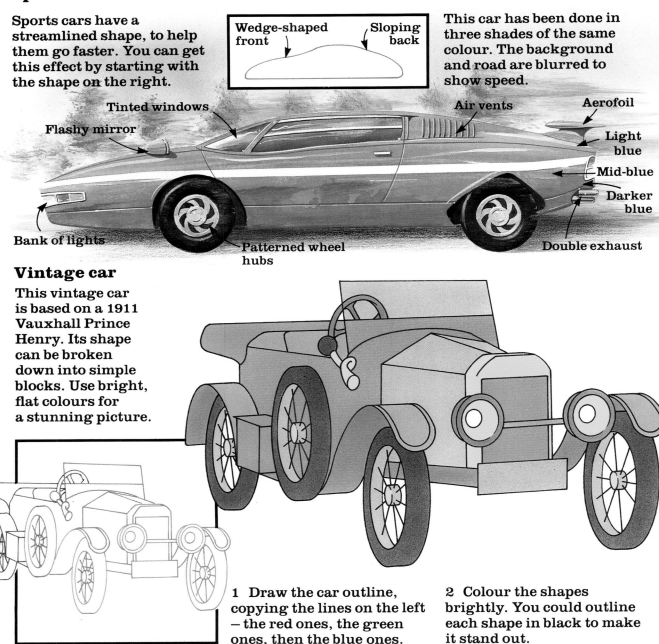

Tinted windows

Flashy mirror

Air vents

Aerofoil

Light blue

Mid-blue

Darker blue

Bank of lights

Patterned wheel hubs

Double exhaust

Vintage car

This vintage car is based on a 1911 Vauxhall Prince Henry. Its shape can be broken down into simple blocks. Use bright, flat colours for a stunning picture.

1 Draw the car outline, copying the lines on the left – the red ones, the green ones, then the blue ones.

2 Colour the shapes brightly. You could outline each shape in black to make it stand out.

Cartoon cars

You can give cars different characters when you draw them as cartoons. Use car parts, such as headlights or the grille to give the car human features such as eyes, mouths and eyebrows. There are some examples of how to do this below.

Draw a friendly car with a round, bright body and wheels bending inwards. You could use the grille as a smiling mouth, the badge as a nose, and the headlights as eyes.

This fierce car has a square, sharp-cornered body and big wheels. Add narrow, shifty eyes and use the front wings as eyebrows. Draw a row of sharp teeth in the grille.

Draw a worn-out car with a dented body, flat tyres, a cracked window and battered paintwork. Make the grille into a sad mouth and turn the headlights into droopy, tired eyes.

Fast and slow

This car looks as if it is speeding round a bend in the road. Draw all the body lines curved, and add curved speed lines to show that the car is moving very fast.

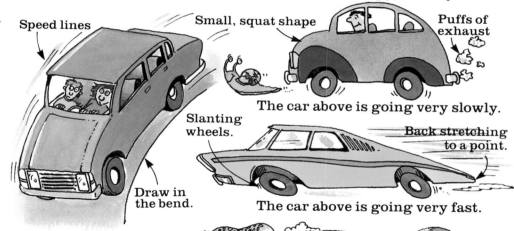

Speed lines

Small, squat shape

Puffs of exhaust

The car above is going very slowly.

Slanting wheels.

Back stretching to a point.

Draw in the bend.

The car above is going very fast.

Crazy cars

Here you can see how to turn the most unlikely objects into cartoon cars.

Big vehicles

On these two pages you can find out how to draw different types of big vehicles such as trucks, tractors and diggers. These are fun to draw because they are made up of big, solid shapes, and you can use bold, bright colours.

Tractor

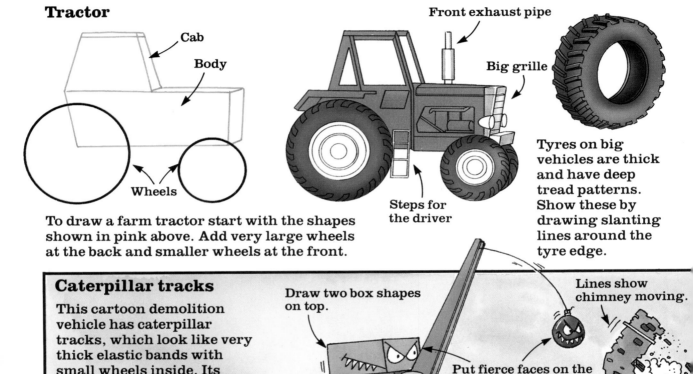

To draw a farm tractor start with the shapes shown in pink above. Add very large wheels at the back and smaller wheels at the front.

Cab

Body

Wheels

Front exhaust pipe

Big grille

Steps for the driver

Tyres on big vehicles are thick and have deep tread patterns. Show these by drawing slanting lines around the tyre edge.

Caterpillar tracks

This cartoon demolition vehicle has caterpillar tracks, which look like very thick elastic bands with small wheels inside. Its body can be broken down into box shapes. See if you can copy it.

Draw two box shapes on top.

Put fierce faces on the vehicle and the ball.

Lines show chimney moving.

Dark shading between inner wheels.

Convoy

You could make a long wall frieze based on the vehicles in the convoy on the right. Copy them freehand, or use a grid to enlarge them as shown on pages 2-3. You could add cars (pages 4-7), motorbikes and bicycles (pages 16-17) to the convoy if you like.

Shading to show ridges.

Shading to show cylinder shape.

Dumper truck

Tanker

Sunset scene

The steps below show you how to draw a scene of a tractor working in a field at sunset. Do the drawing on a large piece of paper. You could use a black felt tip for the outlines in the picture and then colour them in with paints or inks.

Horizon line

Do the sun as a yellow glow, sinking below the horizon.

1 Draw the horizon line in, and paint the sunset above it. Use watery red, orange and yellow paints. Paint the colours in streaks so that they blend together.

Slanting lines show wheel tread pattern.

Spikes for the plough.

2 Draw and colour the tractor in the picture, by copying the shapes above. Do the black shapes first, then the red shapes, then the grey shapes.

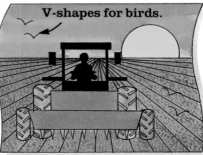

V-shapes for birds.

3 Paint the field brown and speckly. Add lines slanting inwards to the horizon to show the ploughed furrows. Add some V-shaped silhouettes of birds.

Caterpillar tracks move up and down over bumpy ground. Look at the cartoon earthmover on the right to see how to draw them.

You could use windscreen wipers as eyebrows.

Shade inside the shovel.

Horizontal lines across front of caterpillar track.

Curved lines for shovel.

White streaks to make metal shiny.

Long-distance truck

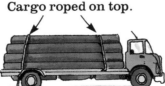

Cargo roped on top.

Four-wheeled flat truck

Shading to show shine on windows.

Articulated lorry

Ships and boats

Here you can see how to draw ships and boats, building them up from simple shapes. There are also some colouring techniques for you to experiment with.

Ship shapes

The shape of an object appears to change, depending on where you are standing when you look at it. This position is called your viewpoint. The horizon is generally level with your viewpoint. Here are some ships seen from different angles.

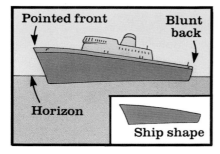

Pointed front — Blunt back — Horizon — Ship shape

To show you are level with the ship, put the horizon line halfway up the picture.

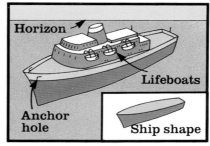

Horizon — Lifeboats — Anchor hole — Ship shape

Put the horizon line near the top to show you are looking down on the ship.

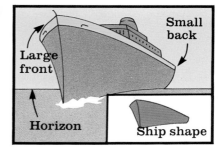

Small back — Large front — Horizon — Ship shape

To show you are looking up at the ship, put the horizon line low.

Night lights

Use wax crayons and blue paint for this cruise liner.

1 Draw the outline in yellow wax on white paper. Put yellow and red reflections in front of the ship.

2 Add portholes along the side of the ship, and some strings of yellow lights.

3 Paint over the whole picture with dark blue paint. It will not stick to the wax, and your ship drawing will show through.

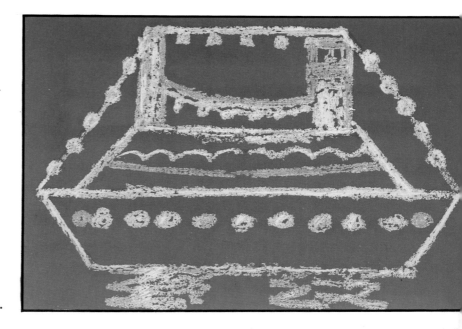

Racing yacht

This racing yacht is done in a sketchy style. Use sharp pencil crayons to scribble on the colours.

1 Draw the yacht outline in faint crayon to start with, copying the shape shown in the box on the right.

2 Scribble in the mast and sail. Scribble stripes on the sails and some people shapes on deck.

3 Go over the hull shape with crayon, missing out the lines behind the sails. Use green and white crayons to scribble in sea.

This crayon style gives the impression of speed and seaspray.

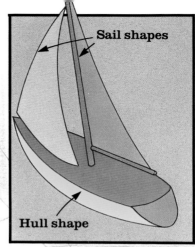

Sail shapes

Hull shape

Sea splashing outwards.

White crayon and bright colours on sails.

Darker colours on hull.

Sea cartoons

Submarine and galleon shapes make good cartoons, as shown below.

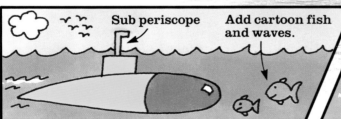

Sub periscope

Add cartoon fish and waves.

Draw someone climbing out of the sub hatch.

Rows of sails

Shield-shaped back

Cannon on sides

Galleon shape

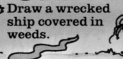

Draw a wrecked ship covered in weeds.

Add a treasure chest.

Snake sea monster

11

Trains

Trains make striking pictures because of their chunky shapes. Here you can see how to draw old-fashioned steam trains and modern high-speed models.

Steam trains

To do a steam train shape, ▶ begin by drawing a cylinder in pencil. Start with an oval and then add two lines and a curve, as shown on the right. Add some wheels at an angle, and join them together with rods. You can then add other extras such as a funnel, buffers, tracks and a driver's cab. Use felt tips for bright, flat colours.

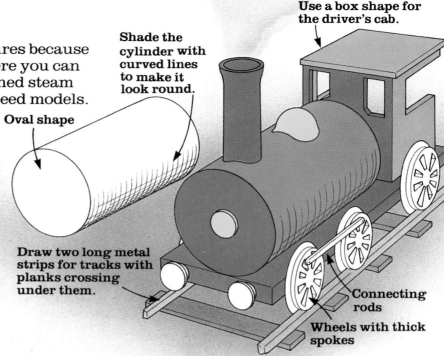

Use a box shape for the driver's cab.

Shade the cylinder with curved lines to make it look round.

Oval shape

Draw two long metal strips for tracks with planks crossing under them.

Connecting rods

Wheels with thick spokes

Use your finger to smudge the charcoal in a curve around the cylinder shape.

Train shape

Smoke and soot

This steam train is drawn in charcoal and chalk for a sooty, smoky look. You can get this effect by following the steps below.

1 Start your picture by sketching the basic train shape with a thin charcoal line. You can copy the shape from the box on the left.

2 Using charcoal, colour the body a light grey and make the shadowy parts darker. Use white chalk to highlight the very shiny parts.

3 Colour in the smoke with chalk and charcoal. Use your finger to smudge them together in circles to get a dramatic billowing effect.*

*You need to fix a charcoal or chalk picture to stop the colour rubbing off (see page 31).

High-speed models

Modern trains are long and streamlined and sometimes have pointed fronts. You don't need to draw wheels on them. A dark shadow under the body gives a good impression of speed.

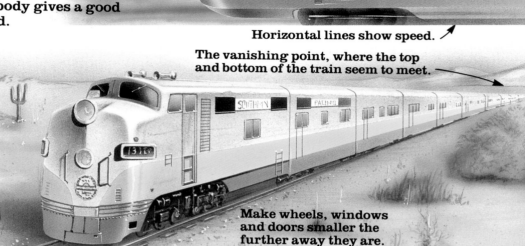

Blurred background

Horizontal lines show speed.

Parts of an object look smaller the further away they are. This is called perspective. A train speeding forwards looks big at the front, and narrows to a point, called the vanishing point, at the back.

The vanishing point, where the top and bottom of the train seem to meet.

SOUTHERN PACIFIC

Make wheels, windows and doors smaller the further away they are.

Trains with brains

You can draw train cartoons by exaggerating the way the trains move, and by giving them human faces. Below are some suggestions.

Lines slanted forwards.

Lines to show braking.

Smoke going the wrong way.

This steam train is dragging a heavy load uphill. Its face looks strained and it is puffing out lots of steam.

This high-speed streamlined train is hurtling downhill. It has a happy face. Draw lots of lines around it to give the idea of speed.

This train is braking hard to avoid a tree on the track. It looks surprised and is squashing itself up and leaning backwards.

Planes

Planes can make spectacular pictures because of their sleek, streamlined shapes. You need to make the surface look shiny on the smooth wings and body.

Plane shape

Speed lines

Exhaust outlet

Use a darker shade beneath the plane.

Cockpit

Pointed nose

You could draw in the ground far below the plane.

Jet plane

1 To draw a jet plane, like the Hawk shown here, start with the long, thin shape, shown in red in the box on the right. Then add wings, shown in blue, and a tailplane, shown in green.

2 Paint or colour the body to give a smooth surface, and add pale highlights to make it look shiny.

Take-off

Follow these three steps to draw a picture of a plane taking off above you.

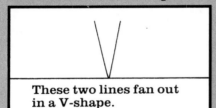

These two lines fan out in a V-shape.

Add building shapes along the horizon.

1 Draw a horizon line across the paper. In faint pencil draw two straight lines fanning out from the centre of the horizon line. Use a ruler to help you get an accurate shape.

2 Draw the plane as shown above, using the lines fanning outwards as the sides of the plane body. Colour it in, adding silhouettes of the airport on the horizon.

3 Draw lines fanning out towards you, for the runway. Add white star shapes along each of the lines to show the runway lights. Make the stars bigger towards the front.

14

Formation flying

To draw a formation flying team repeat the plane outline shown in the box on the right several times, in any flying pattern you like. You could draw your picture on a bright blue background with trails of different coloured smoke behind the planes.

Draw smoke trails with a series of curves, like this.

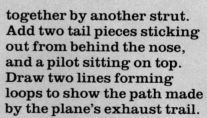

Use one bright team colour for the plane shapes.

Plane shape

Sky writer

This cartoon sky-writing plane has a round body and a fat tail and wings. Add a cheerful face and a black nose. Make its smoke trail spell a word or show a pattern of curls and twists.

Bi-plane

Start this picture of a bi-plane by drawing a triangular nose. Then add the wings, with struts and pieces of wire criss-crossed between them. Add the wheels, which are joined

together by another strut. Add two tail pieces sticking out from behind the nose, and a pilot sitting on top. Draw two lines forming loops to show the path made by the plane's exhaust trail.

Turn your plane upside down to make it look like an aerobatic stunt.

Draw in a bird to show the right way up.

15

Bicycles and motorbikes

Bicycle shapes are quite complicated so it is a good idea to do a pencil sketch of your drawing first. Once you have got the shape right you can colour it in.

On these pages you can see how to draw action-packed pictures of bicycles and motorbikes and how to give them a professional finish.

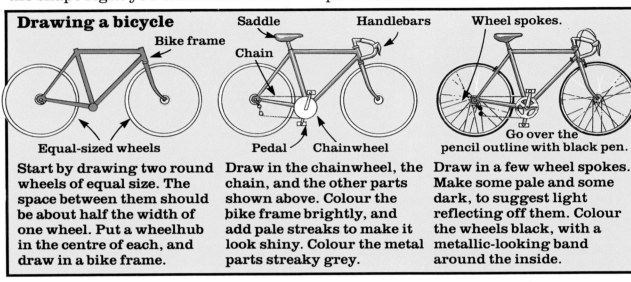

Drawing a bicycle

Bike frame

Saddle

Handlebars

Wheel spokes.

Chain

Pedal

Chainwheel

Equal-sized wheels

Go over the pencil outline with black pen.

Start by drawing two round wheels of equal size. The space between them should be about half the width of one wheel. Put a wheelhub in the centre of each, and draw in a bike frame.

Draw in the chainwheel, the chain, and the other parts shown above. Colour the bike frame brightly, and add pale streaks to make it look shiny. Colour the metal parts streaky grey.

Draw in a few wheel spokes. Make some pale and some dark, to suggest light reflecting off them. Colour the wheels black, with a metallic-looking band around the inside.

People on bikes

Here are some pictures of people riding bikes. The stick figures drawn in red are to help you draw the people in the right position. Do the stick figures in light pencil and then gradually build up the body shapes around them.

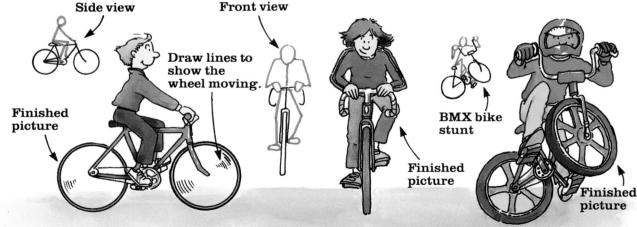

Side view

Front view

Draw lines to show the wheel moving.

Finished picture

BMX bike stunt

Finished picture

Finished picture

Motorbikes

To do a picture of a shiny, streamlined motorbike follow the three steps here.

1 Use the grid method on pages 2-3 to copy the motorbike's main shapes.

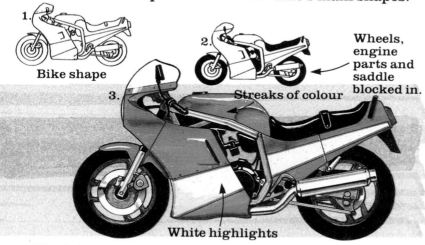

1. Bike shape

2. Wheels, engine parts and saddle blocked in.

3. Streaks of colour

White highlights

2 Block in the dark areas with one dark colour.
3 You can make the paintwork look shiny by shading it in streaks, using felt tip pens in three or four shades of the same colour. Leave the shiniest part of the body white, or paint on white highlights.

Super-shine

For a super-shiny look draw a motorbike outline in white pencil crayon on black paper. Shade in the shiniest parts and leave the rest of the bike black.

Fun bikes

Lines to show shaking.

This cartoon bike is being ridden over rough ground. It is drawn with a wiggly outline.

Start this dragster with a triangle shape. The rider has to lean back a long way in the seat.

Speed lines

The basic shape of a rider seen from behind is similar to the front view shown on page 16.

Robots

You can have fun drawing robots because they can be any shape, size or colour you like. Below are some ideas for robot pictures to start you off.

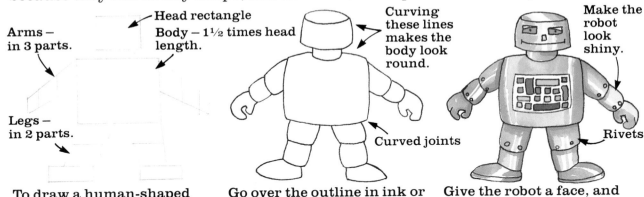

Arms – in 3 parts.

Head rectangle
Body – 1½ times head length.

Legs – in 2 parts.

Curving these lines makes the body look round.

Curved joints

Make the robot look shiny.

Rivets

To draw a human-shaped robot, first do a pencil sketch, using simple block shapes to get the size right.

Go over the outline in ink or felt pen, making the body rounder. Rub out pencil marks and colour the robot.

Give the robot a face, and put a control panel covered in knobs on its chest. Add some dots for rivets.

Robot assortment

You can use all kinds of shapes to draw robots. Below is an assortment of heads, bodies and legs. You could copy or trace these parts, and mix and match them to make up your own robot. Use bright colours and any other extras you like.

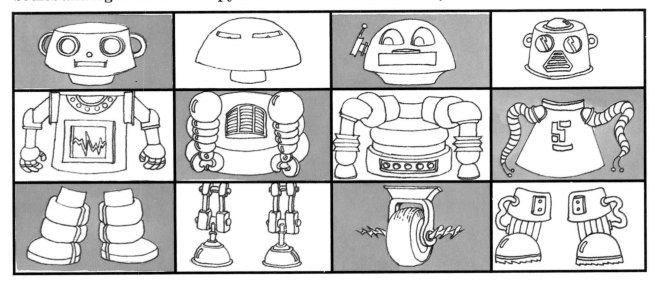

Special robots

Drawing this robot from below makes it look bigger and fiercer. The body gets narrower as it gets further away.

You could try designing a robot to do a special job. This robot has nine arms so it can do lots of household chores at once.

This robot has gone wrong. Its arms and legs are out of control, and there are electric sparks coming out of its control panel.

Hooked hands

Draw big feet.

Crazy eyes

Zigzags and stars to show electric sparks.

Robots you know

Here you can see how to make some of the people and animals you know look like robots. Give them robot bodies but add features so they can be recognized.

Granny robot

Teacher robot

Cat robot

Dog robot

Robot t-shirt

Robot control

Press here

Decorate a white t-shirt with a robot control panel. You will need to use special pens which you can buy for colouring on fabric.

Space machines

On the next four pages there are lots of space machine drawings for you to try, using wax and pencil crayons, paints or felt tips.

Shuttle launch

To draw this dramatic space shuttle launch follow the steps below.

1 Draw the launch in three stages, copying the outline on the right. Do the plane-shaped part first, then the fuel tank, then the two rocket boosters.

2 Crayon or paint the shuttle. Streak the colours or add white highlights to make it look shiny.

3 Colour in a cloud of exhaust all around the shuttle, using white, yellow, orange, red and grey.

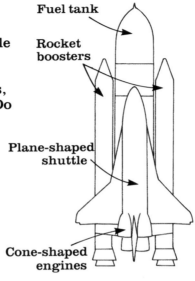

Fuel tank

Rocket boosters

Plane-shaped shuttle

Cone-shaped engines

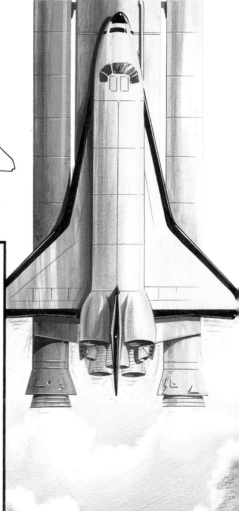

Out in space

You could try drawing rockets and planets on white paper, using brightly coloured wax crayon. Then wash over the whole picture with black paint*.

When it is dry, you can add bright stars. Dip an old toothbrush in white paint. Hold it bristles-down over the paper and run your finger towards you along the bristles.

*Tape the picture down on a flat surface while the paint dries, to stop it crinkling.

On the Moon

Here you can see how to draw a picture of the Apollo 11 Lunar Module, the first spacecraft to put a man on the Moon.

1 Use the grid method on pages 2-3 to copy the outline shown in red below.

Module shape

This Lunar Module landed on the Moon on 20 July 1969.

2 Paint the bottom section to look like reflective gold foil, by splodging on yellow, orange and white watercolour paint, so that the colours run together.

3 Paint the top section grey, with shiny-looking white parts and dark shadowy lines to suggest equipment shapes. Paint in the legs and the ladder.

4 Paint the moonscape in shades of grey, with crater shapes. You could add footprints coming from the craft. Paint the sky black, with stars.

Space station

To draw this space station start with the outline below.

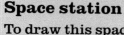

Colour in the space station, and add the parts labelled.

To draw the spacewalking astronaut, start with lots of circle shapes, as shown on the right. Then draw a body outline round the circles.

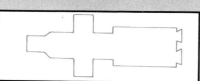

Astronaut shape

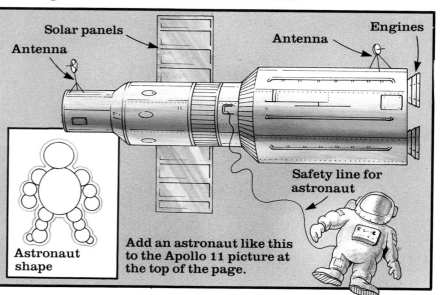

Solar panels

Antenna

Antenna

Engines

Safety line for astronaut

Add an astronaut like this to the Apollo 11 picture at the top of the page.

Alien spaceships

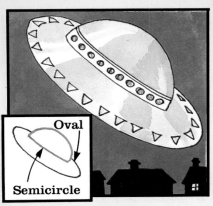

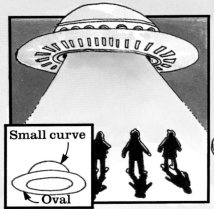

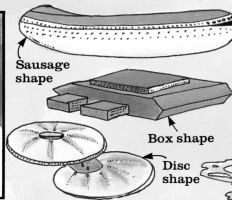

Sausage shape

Box shape

Disc shape

Oval

Semicircle

Small curve

Oval

This flying saucer has arrived over Earth. Its shape is made up of part of a circle and part of an oval. Add round windows, triangular lights, and a row of houses below.

This flying saucer is taking off from Earth after a visit. Draw an oval, with a small curve on top to show the roof. Add coloured rays coming out from the bottom of the saucer.

Alien spaceships do not have to be saucer-shaped. You can use any shape you like, and add extras to it such as windows and flashing lights. There are some suggestions above.

Space city

The shapes of the space machines in this science-fiction city are shown in the box on the opposite page. You could copy them and colour them any way you like. Build up a space scene with futuristic plants and houses in the background.

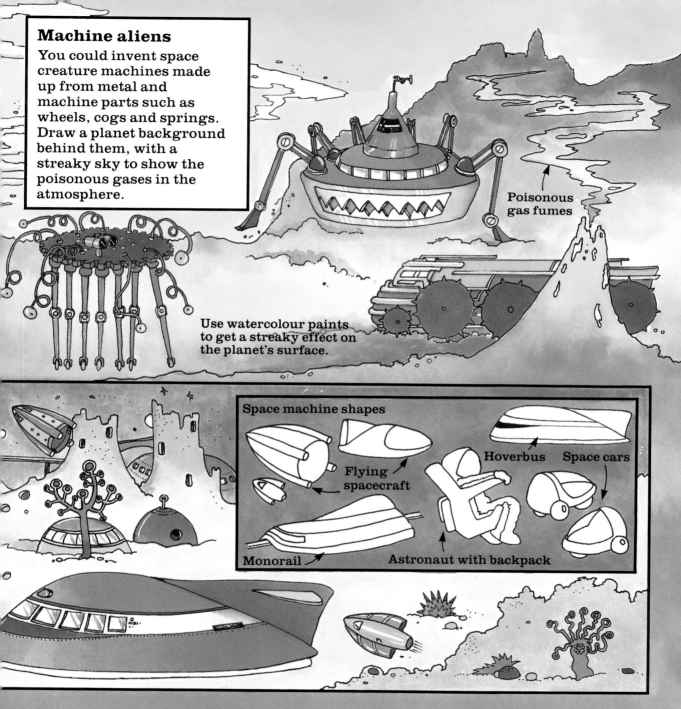

Machine aliens

You could invent space creature machines made up from metal and machine parts such as wheels, cogs and springs. Draw a planet background behind them, with a streaky sky to show the poisonous gases in the atmosphere.

Poisonous gas fumes

Use watercolour paints to get a streaky effect on the planet's surface.

Space machine shapes

Flying spacecraft

Hoverbus

Space cars

Monorail

Astronaut with backpack

23

Batty inventions

Before you draw your own batty invention, first decide what job you want it to do. On these pages are some ideas to start you off, showing you how to make your machines work using parts such as cogs, wheels and rivets.

Heath Robinson

Heath Robinson was a famous illustrator of the 1930s. He was especially well-known for his pictures of amazing inventions. He made them up using lots of objects joined together in unexpected ways. Each invention was designed to do a special job. The picture on the right is a Heath Robinson idea for a potato peeling machine*.

Trying it yourself

You could try drawing your own invention using everyday bits and pieces joined together in original ways.

Draw in arrows and labels to show how the parts fit together.

Blueprint

Blueprints are photographic copies of designs. These may be given to the manufacturers of a machine, to show how all its parts fit together.

To make a drawing look like a blueprint do it as an outline in dark blue pencil crayon, on pale blue paper.

Tea pourer

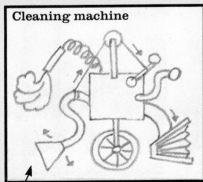

Cleaning machine

Blueprints

*Reproduced by kind permission of The Estate of Mrs J.C. Robinson.

Plant waterer

The plant waterer on the right uses rope, a see-saw, springs, cogs and balls to make the watering can tip over and water the flowers. You could try adapting this idea to make it into a shower spray attached to the bath. There is also an idea for a machine which butters toast on the front cover of this book.

Wind this way.

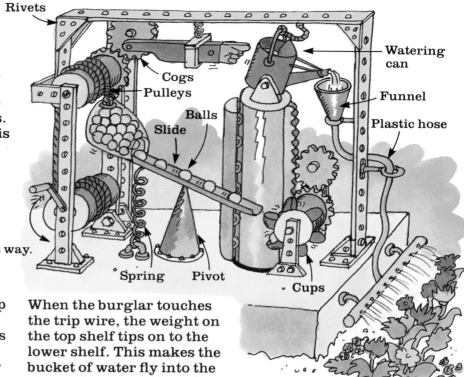

Rivets

Watering can

Cogs

Pulleys

Funnel

Plastic hose

Balls

Slide

Spring

Pivot

Cups

Burglar trap

This idea for a burglar trap is quite simple to draw. It uses wire, weights, shelves and a bucket of water. You could hide the wire among some plants.

When the burglar touches the trip wire, the weight on the top shelf tips on to the lower shelf. This makes the bucket of water fly into the air and land on the burglar.

Weight

Rod

Pivot

Shelf

Bucket

Trip wire

IDEAS LIST

Here are some other suggestions for you to try:

MORNING ALARM
SEED PLANTER
SHOWER SPRAY
PET FEEDER

Drawing from life

To do an accurate drawing of a machine that is in front of you, look at it carefully. Note how wide it is compared to how high it is, and how its different parts compare to each other in size. These sizes are called proportions.

Check the proportions by using your thumb and a pencil as shown below.

1 With one eye closed, hold a pencil out at arm's length. Line up the pencil with one of the edges on the object.

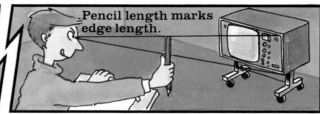

2 Mark the length of the edge, by positioning your thumb at the bottom, and the pencil end at the top.

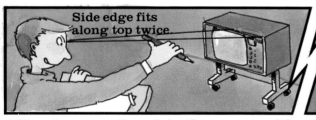

3 Keeping your thumb in the same position, check how many times this length fits into other parts of the object.

4 Check that the proportions in your drawing compare to each other in a similar way. If they do not, alter your sketch.

Shadows

To get the shadows in the right place on a realistic picture, first see which direction the light is coming from. Then put shadows on areas that are hidden from the light.

Don't forget to show background shadows around any objects you draw. This makes a picture look more realistic*.

Light coming from this way.

These parts are hidden from the light.

Shadow thrown on a table.

26 *Different sorts of shading are shown on page 3.

Designing real machines

Engineering designers sketch out their ideas on paper, to help them decide how to build a machine and what it should look like. They try out many ideas before deciding on the best one. On the next few pages there are tips on how they develop a new product, and how you can design your own machine.

Design steps

Here you can see how a designer might develop an idea for a new-style kettle. Follow the three steps below to draw up your own idea for a machine which would be useful. Bear in mind the checklist on the right.

2 Draw this shape bigger ▶ and work out how the different parts will fit together.

◀ 1 Sketch out different shapes and choose the best one.

Designer's checklist

Ask yourself these questions before you design your machine.

What do you want it to do?

How can you make it work efficiently?

How can you make it safe?

How can you make it easy to use?

How can you make it look attractive?

House improvements

You could try to redesign some of the machines in your house, thinking of ways to make them more efficient, practical or attractive. Here are some ideas.

New stereo system with TV incorporated

New toaster design

New-style telephone

New-style deckchair

3 Finish off your ▶ picture by colouring it in, to make it look more attractive. Rub out any pencil lines that are still showing at the end. Label the different parts of the machine clearly.

Wide spout for easy pouring.

Hinged top for easy filling.

Wide, stable base.

Strong handle

Computer graphics

Engineers sometimes use computers to help them design machines. This process is called CAD (computer-aided design). They work out measurements which they feed into the computer, so that it produces a simple line drawing of a machine structure.

You can do a picture that looks like a computer design. Draw a machine shape in brightly-coloured lines on a paler background. This computer graphics space shuttle is done with fine felt tips on coloured paper.

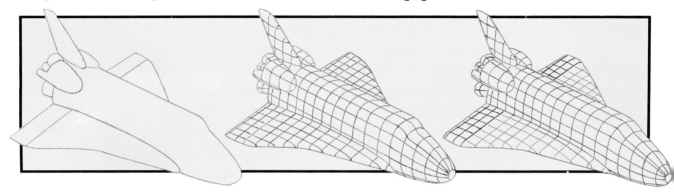

1 Draw the outline of the body in a bright colour.

2 Draw in lines following the contours of the body.

You could use different colours for different parts.

Blow-ups

Designers often use a "blow-up" technique to enlarge one part of a machine and show it in detail.

1 To do a blow-up, draw the whole machine first. Don't colour it in yet.

2 Draw two lines coming from the part you want to enlarge, and a big circle or square.

3 Draw the part bigger and in more detail inside the circle, then colour the whole picture.

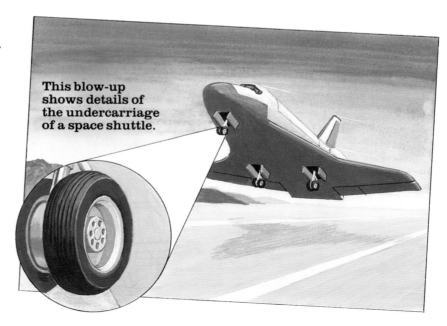

This blow-up shows details of the undercarriage of a space shuttle.

Exploded drawing

This futuristic car design is done as an exploded drawing. The technique is used by designers to show where the different parts of a machine fit, by drawing them hovering near their true position. Follow the steps below to do the picture.

1 To draw the car body shape, shown below, start with the blue lines.

Arrows show where parts are supposed to fit.

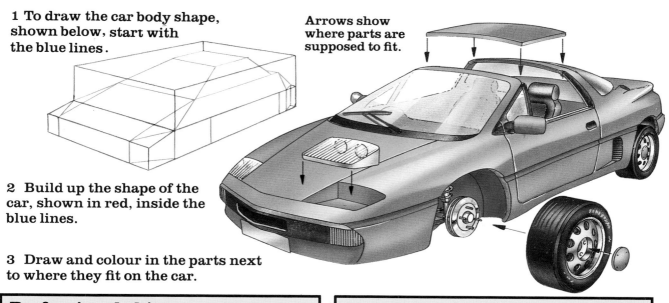

2 Build up the shape of the car, shown in red, inside the blue lines.

3 Draw and colour in the parts next to where they fit on the car.

Professional shine

Artists sometimes use an airbrush to get a smooth effect on machine pictures. This is a device for spraying paint or ink out of a fine nozzle. Before spraying one part of the picture all the rest is protected with a "mask" made from card or masking film. The car drawing above is airbrushed.

Airbrush

Mask

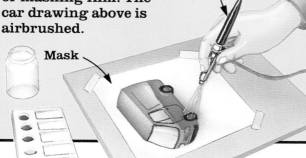

Avoiding smudges

Charcoal, chalk and soft pencil smudge easily. You can stop this by spraying a fixative over your finished picture. Art shops sell fixative spray in aerosol cans. It is dangerous to breathe it in so always use it in a well-ventilated area. It should never be used near a flame.

Cutaway pictures

In cutaway pictures, part of a machine's outer casing is cut away to show the inside. This style can give a clear idea of how a machine works.

On these pages you can find out how to draw cutaways of real machines, and there are some ideas for making up your own imaginary cutaways.

Step-by-step cutaway

Here you can see how to draw a cutaway of a bicycle light. To copy machine workings accurately, you need to see them. Bicycle lights are quite easy to take apart safely.*

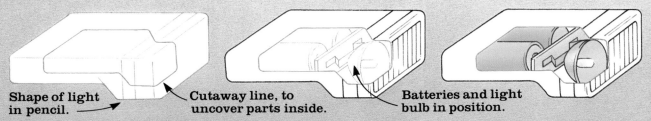

Shape of light in pencil.

Cutaway line, to uncover parts inside.

Batteries and light bulb in position.

1 Pencil in the outer shape of the machine. Draw a line to show the edge of the section that you want to cut away.

2 Draw the machine parts inside the section you have cut away. Go around the parts and the body outline with felt pen or ink.

3 You could colour in the machine parts, but leave the outer shell black and white, as shown above. Rub out any pencil marks.

Car cutaway

You can do this picture by looking under a car bonnet or at a car manual.

1 Draw the car shape (see page 4).

2 Draw a cutaway line round a section of the bonnet, and draw the machinery inside.

3 To show the difference between the inside and outside you could colour in the car body, and simply outline the parts.

You can simplify the shapes of the machine parts.

Leave part of the bonnet on.

*Always take machines apart carefully. Make sure you do not cancel any guarantee by dismantling parts.

Made-up cutaways

You could try drawing a machine cutaway and making up the insides yourself. The parts you draw don't have to be realistic. There are some examples to try below.

Robot

Try doing a robot cutaway. Use the shape on page 18. Then cut away part of the robot's body to show the inner workings. This robot has cogs, wheels and wires inside its control panel. You could also draw a scientist adjusting them.

Telephone

There are tiny people inside this cutaway of a telephone. One is listening to the incoming call, one is taking the message down, and one is shouting it out through the earpiece. Try making up cutaway pictures of machines around your home, showing people busy working inside them.

Big machines

Big machines make good cutaways. Try drawing an aeroplane, a train, or a space station like the one shown below (see page 21 for the shape). Cut away part of the body to show the people and equipment inside.

People shapes

To draw cartoon people to go inside a machine, follow the steps below.

1 Start with a body and head shape.

2 Add arms, legs, hands and feet.

3 Add details, like clothes and a face.

Index

First published in 1987 by Usborne Publishing Ltd,
20 Garrick Street, London WC2E 9BJ, England.

Copyright © Usborne Publishing Ltd, 1987

The name Usborne and the device ♈ are Trade Marks of
Usborne Publishing Ltd.